Loser Of The Year

A Collection of Quiet Failures & Loud Feelings

Priyanka Samadhan

Made with ❤ on the BookLeaf Publishing Platform
www.bookleafpub.in
www.bookleafpub.com

Dedication

To you,
who have failed sincerely,
given up with grace.

I write for the ones who do not run marathons
but do walk in emotional circles,
who do not chase greatness
but politely step aside to let it pass.

To those who did not win,
did not shine,
did not "make the most of it."

This is for you.
The quietly collapsing, the tenderly tired.
You may not have triumphed,
but you endured.

And that, perhaps, is its own kind of poetry.

Preface

I did not mean to write this book.

For years, I tried to write the kind of book I dreamed of publishing. Not once did I finish the first draft. *Not once.* Each attempt quietly collapsed under the weight of my own ambition, or procrastination, or whatever invisible force it is that keeps people like me circling the idea instead of landing it.

And then came this strange little concept. A book about failure. A collection of poems for the not-quite-there, the socially exhausted, the emotionally overcommitted and professionally underwhelming.

Naturally, I doubted I could finish it.
But I did. Surprisingly.
And if this book ever gets read by anyone at all it shall be my first true accomplishment.

Thank you for picking this up. Even if by accident.
Especially if by accident.
I am deeply grateful you are here.

Acknowledgements

There is usually a long list of people to thank here. Mentors, friends, muses, editors, baristas. But in the making of this book, it was just me with a stubborn idea that refused to leave.

So I must thank what truly deserves it: the silence, the overthinking, the oddly comforting chaos of solitude, the circumstances I did not ask for, the strangers I barely knew, and the moments that bruised and bewildered me. You built the landscape where these words took root.

And of course, **Book Leaf Publishing**, thank you for the writing challenge that unknowingly cornered me into finally finishing something. Without that odd pressure, this book might still be a *someday.*

If you are reading this, know that even the most unaccompanied journeys can lead somewhere. This one led here.

From one quiet failure to another: thank you for reading.

1. Loser's Manual

Step one:
Arrive late,
not out of disregard,
not from laziness,
but because your wiring is
a slow, unsynchronized beat,
and the world never waited for it.
Mess things up,
not with malice,
but with that strange grace
of breaking rules
by merely breathing wrong.

Step two:
Apologize for your very existence,
especially in the group photo,
Stand in the back.
Laugh too late.
Say "you too" when someone says "Happy birthday."

Step three:
Collect dreams like souvenirs
borrowed from faraway places
you will never visit.

Too many to hold,
too fragile to finish.
Stacked like receipts,
crumpled, unread,
faded by the time
you finally need them.

Step four:
Let someone love you.
Then disappear,
Because staying feels like acting.
Affection sounds scripted.
Leave,
because fading is far easier
than being anything at all.

Step five:
Do not let them
hear you cry in the bathroom.
Learn that losing
is never loud.
It is quiet.
It is missing a call
you were too scared to answer.
It is deleting a draft
you almost believed in.
It is watching them look at you

like you have become
a person they pity.

Final step:
Repeat until it feels like home.

Congratulations.
You're not a villain,
not a hero.

You are,
simply,
a loser
through and through.

Welcome to the story.

2. Not the Main Character

I am not the protagonist.
And truly, what a relief.

The city bustles.
People run, shout, kiss, cry.
I sip cold coffee by the window.
I do not intervene.

Someone drops a wallet.
Someone proposes.
Someone shouts into their phone.
Friends argue two tables over.
One storms out.
The other lights a cigarette.

A cab splashes a puddle onto a woman in heels.
She laughs too loudly.
Her friend pulls her into a selfie.
I smile into my coffee cup.

At the station,
lovers say goodbye like it is the end of the world.
I miss my ride
and do not mind.

They will remember today.
I will not.
I will fold it quietly
into the drawer of ordinary days.

I have long accepted my lack of plot.
No tragic backstory?
No sweeping romance?
No prophetic destiny?
Splendid.

Not the main character?
Yes.
And thank God.

Because someone must witness
without needing to be seen.

And who better than a *loser*
who never asked to win?

3. Noise Cancelling

The room is loud.
but only in my head.

Outside: a fan performs
its monotone aria,
the fridge sighs
like a lonely philosopher
and someone, somewhere,
is performing
a dramatic monologue
about the weather.

I nod,
like I understand.
A world-class mimic of engagement.
A trained listener.

My words...
God, my words.
They do not walk out of me
like civilized guests.
They pace.
Hostages behind my teeth,
negotiating for better conditions.

Someone,
bright-eyed and harmless,
smiles and says,
"you're so quiet."
Thank you.
It is either this
or a full-scale meltdown.

It's not that I do not have things to say.
I have *too much*.
A thesis on despair,
a comedy of self-loathing,
a whole opera
on the absurdity of waking up every day
like it means something.
But none of that
goes well with coffee..

So instead,
I give a nod.
A diplomatic "mmhm."
Smile like it does not cost me blood..

It is not shyness.
Shyness implies
a desire to be louder.

No.
It is preservation.
It is choosing not to bleed.

I am noise cancelling.
That is all.

4. When Words Wear Disguises

He said
"don't quit your day job"
and I, like a fool,
nodded.
Grateful,
for the advice from a friend.

But the words
hung in the air.
I did not know
it was meant like a jab
wrapped in a joke.

They speak in riddles,
these people.
Their voices dancing
around meanings I cannot catch,
and by the time I catch up,
the map has changed,
and I am lost again.
Each phrase a trapdoor.

And I,

always I,
am left standing
at the border
between "what is said"
and "what is meant."

I do not speak in irony.
I do not whisper in winks.
I do not lace my truths
in invisible ink.
I take words
like water–
direct, necessary.
like water from a well
with no flavor but thirst.

But here,
language is layered
like cake.
Everyone's eating the icing
while I chewed the cardboard beneath.

They tell me,
"Lighten up, it's a joke."
A joke?
To me, it felt like
a small betrayal

with good lighting.

Sometimes i wonder
if it's *me*,
if my mind missed a memo
when it was learning
how people mean things
without saying them.

So,
I sit quietly.
I smile,
which is what you do
when your understanding
runs out
but the conversation does not.

The room hums with meanings
I will never know.
And my words?
My poor, unshapely, honest words...
fall like stones.

5. The Anatomy of Asking

My stomach,
a tragic heroine,
flinging herself
off the ledge
like a fool
auditioning for martyrdom
at the beep of a notification.
She knows no chill,
when the message pops "can we talk?"

My heart?
God bless her,
tap dancing in combat boots,
boom, boom,
badum,
BOOM
because I dared to ask,
"Can I borrow some money?"
As though I had not practiced it
like a Shakespearean death monologue
in the shower
for three consecutive nights.

Meanwhile, my palms sweat

as if I had been summoned
to testify
for crimes I have not committed,
when I whisper
a dream I have kept in my lungs
like contraband.

Asking for permission
to live the life I already own
feels illegal.
I write the words down.
Rehearse them.
Again. Again.
Again.

My throat?
A clogged funnel of feelings.
Words pile up like prisoners.
None make it out.
Some riot.
Most dissolve.
One says "never mind"
and leaves because
choking is not worth it.

And upstairs,
my brain hosts a conference.

Topic:
"Why You Will Be Rejected,
Humiliated,
And Publicly Shamed."
She has charts.
She has graphs.
She has a slideshow
featuring the time
I cried in a stationery shop.

Some people leap.
I...tremble, trip, type and delete.

At least my organs
are excellent performers.

6. Socially Unavailable

Ah, the people.
Those faces I know, sort of,
or maybe they know me.
We talk, but not really.
They speak, terribly loud.

I sip water like it is a potion of confidence,
calculating if my one sentence
about the weather
is worth slicing through the noise.

Once, I was loud.
I would interrupt myself
just to say something funnier.

Now, I run a full internal monologue
before forming one socially acceptable sentence.
I try to speak,
but then my words are late to the party,
the guffaws already spilled
and the room filled with someone else's shine.

It is easier to disappear.
I slide into the background

a shadow among cushions,
a leaf among houseplants.

Somewhere along the way,
I turned down the volume
and no one noticed.
Not even *me.*
Until silence, sweet silence,
felt like second skin.

But here I am.
In the corner, a mere oddity,
half wallflower,
half failure,
flourishing in my own way,
quietly, absurdly,
too polite, too aware.

7. Left on Read, But Relieved

The last message remains...
unsentenced.
A digital relic.
A fossilized moment
I once thought
might resurrect me.
But it did not sink.
It did not soar.
It simply... stayed.
Flat.
Like my expectations

And I..
I thought I would die
if silence answered back.
I thought my entire sense of self
depended
on a stupid ping
or three dots bubbling in anticipation.

But now..
now there is silence,
and I'm still here.
Incredibly alive.

Painfully alive.

The anxiety that bubbled in my chest,
the texts I read and reread,
looking for meaning
where there was none.
All of it has
washed away,
quiet as an afterthought.

There was a time
I combed through messages
with the scrutiny of an old monk
decoding holy scripture.

Every period
was a punishment.
Every "lol"
a cryptic prophecy.
Do they hate me?
Are they mocking me?
Did my joke
cause a mild existential crisis
on their end?

Now, I feel the peace
settling in.

And dare I say
it is better this way.
To not be half-held
by half-conversations.

To not be strung along
by ellipses
and the cruel theatre
of typing bubbles.

Maybe I have grown,
or maybe I have numbed.
Hard to say.
Growth and numbness
wear the same coat in winter.

But I'm okay.
More than okay.

And somehow,
it is better this way.
A world where messages
do not *rule* my heart.

8. A Textual Tragedy

hey,
I began like an idiot.
Even in lowercase, it felt too forward.
I erased it.

sorry for the late reply–
What a coward's anthem.

just saw your message!
Lie. I saw it.
I watched it sit there.
Three days ago.
Twice.
At work.
In bed.
On the toilet.

Was gonna text you back but–
... lol nvm.
That sentence never makes it out alive.
Like most of me.

hi
That sounds weird.

Too abrupt.
Too casual.
Too desperate.

i was thinking about what you said,
and honestly–

…
There is no "honestly" left in me.
Forget it.

you still up?
Unsent. Of course.
Because what if you are?
And worse, what if you are not?

i hope you're doing–
And here the sentence dies.
Because I no longer know what you are doing.

let's hangout soon. I miss–
No. That is not the truth.
I would rather nap.
You understand, right?

just wanted to say
thanks
(or sorry?)

(or both?)
Why does everything I feel
require a disclaimer?

maybe we could–
Never mind.

Read 2:03 AM

I will reply when I am
less tired.
Less alive
in this bruised way
that makes every word
a small tragedy
of intention.

9. Plot > People

I did not weep,
when we drifted apart
or when we stopped being "us"
whatever *that* meant.
Just a ghost of a connection.
A dying bond.

But when Ace died..
Oh, God.
I was inconsolable.
Red-eyed, ugly sobbing.
Luffy screamed
and so did I,
across screens,
across universes,
both of us
betrayed by fire and fate.

And still,
some smug voice asks,
"how can you cry over fiction?"
As though their group chats
hold deeper truths.
As though their midnight gossip

bears more substance.

In real life,
someone shrugs
and says "take care,"
and that's the end of your era.
The mundane cycle of life,
feels pointless,
too superficial.

but fiction..
fiction grabs my hand,
drags me through storm and sea,
and leaves me
shattered and whole
at the same time.

In books and stories,
grief has purpose,
sacrifice has music,
love is loud,
people mean what they say.

I have been called heartless
for not mourning
over a friendship turned husk.

But tell me..
Would you ache for a poem
that never found its ending?

Had we shared one *real* moment,
just one,
I would still be rewinding it.

10. Heard You Think I'm Holy

They call me sweet.
God help me.
I merely nodded
and smiled perhaps.
Like I have subscribed
to their life updates.

But I am not nice.
Not in the sacred, beatific sense.

You recount, for the third time,
your theory on late-stage capitalism.
I listen not because I care,
but because I lack the stamina
to add my deflated opinion
to another inflated topic.

I do not think my brain can handle the burnout
from debating things that evaporate
in a blink.

You say I am a good listener.
But I am just.. conserving energy.

Because truly,
most conversations feel like
bubble wrap.
Soft, satisfying,
and ultimately... empty.

Will I speak?
Certainly.
If it is a matter of life or death.
Yours, mine, or
a fictional character's.

I am no saint either.
I have sinned quietly.
In the background.
Off-screen.
I have lied.
I have googled "how to be a better person"
at 2:36 AM
only to close the tab.

The guilt, you ask?
It follows me
like a library book overdue by years.
I cannot return it.
I will not throw it away.
It's mine now.

We live together in silence.

So when you say,
"You're so nice,"
I flinch.
Not because it's wrong,
but because it's *too* wrong.
You are mistaken.
Profoundly.

I am not cruel.
I am just…
a little morally ambiguous
and very discreet about it.

11. College Ghost

12:43 PM
Lunch break.
A half-eaten dosa,
two fake laughs,
And a sudden,
unshakable craving
for escape.

1:12 PM
I walked out after lunch.
Left my ID in the canteen.
Texted a friend "brb."
It's been 2 years.
No one followed up.
Which, in a way,
was the kindest closure.

2:25 PM
Somewhere between
the third semester and
my third identity crisis,
I understood
no curriculum
was designed

to fix me,
a person slowly imploding.
And, I did not care
if Socrates had opinions
about it either.

[Weeks Missing]

Group projects still marked me "active."
Quiet.
Politely absent.
I became the ghost no one noticed until
the attendance sheet whispered my name like an ex.

[Today]

Sometimes I google the college
just to confirm it did not crumble
without my emotional support.
It did not.
Of course it did not.
Buildings do not miss people.

[Somewhere in the Future]

No degree.
No convocation photo.
But a peculiar kind of peace
that no classroom offered.

And if the world
spun calmly
without me graduating,
Then maybe,
just maybe..
I was never the crack
in the system.

Just a *misfit*
who left.

12. Professional Quitter

I am twenty-five,
and already
a practiced deserter.
A saboteur of my own beginnings.
A seasoned escape artist.

Resume includes:
- 3 jobs ghosted
- 2 hobbies abandoned
- 1 therapist left on read
- countless unread books

I quit diets, drama,
deadlines, dreams.
I do not rebel.
I simply... excuse myself.
At the first sign of resistance,
I vanish.
Quietly. Without scandal.

Poof.

They call it giving up.
I call it strategic withdrawal

from the battlefield of expectation.
I am allergic to ambition.
Dreams itch.

I do not know how to break the pattern.
A circle walked so many times.
They say I lack direction.
I say I possess too many
and follow none.

Perhaps quitting is my one true calling.
Consistency disguised as failure.
A rhythm made of exits.

Either way...
here's to giving up,
early and often,
like a true professional.

Print it on a mug.
Stamp it on a tote.
Place it beside my faded dreams,
 gathering dust
on the shelf I meant to build
 but never quite did.

13. The Grocery List

To buy:

- Eggs

- Milk

- Bananas (Because I was supposed to eat healthy, but who cares?)

- Cheese (For emotional support.)

- Soap (For hands and perhaps the stubborn stains of shame.)

- Something green (To pretend I have my life together.)

- Tissue box (For allergies. Yes. That is all.)

- Chocolate (Do not ask, just get it.)

- Cello tape (To hold the crumbling façade together.)

- A packet of anxiety pills (No, just kidding. But the thought was sincere, and lingered.)

- Motivation (Not in the top shelf. Not in the bottom either.)

- Purpose (Out of stock)

- Silence (Unsurprisingly loud)

- A refund for the last 48 hours

- A clone (To attend that thing for me.)

- A break

- A breakdown

- A therapist

- A teleportation device

- A sign from the universe

- A hug (optional)

-

-

- And lastly, *Me.* (Not the older model. Just me, updated. With fewer bugs.)

14. Accidental Villain Arc

I snapped once..
A quiet declaration:
"I can't do this right now."

And thus began my descent
into the role of antagonist.

I did not slam doors,
I ceased to nod,
ceased to agree
to things that hollowed me.

Yet suddenly,
I became
a rogue variable in their equation.
Saitama, on a laundry day,
stripped off irony,
Loki in a hoodie,
rebellious and defiant.

They did not see the prelude.
The lip bitten raw,
the stare fixed on the floor,
as though it might offer counsel,

the silent war waged
in the notes app.

I am not plotting,
I am merely processing,
on a lagging system.

I am not cold,
just crispy from overuse.
I am not evil,
just...
a little done for today.

It is not villainy
to be tired.
Nor heresy,
to need silence.
I have been decorating
my emptiness
with humor
and memes
since 2016.

So if you see me
walk off
with a certain theatrical sadness,
let me.

Even villains
must stand before the mirror
to dab at a single tear,
and try desperately
to remember
the original plot.

15. The Disappointed Look

There it is again..
The Look.
Not fury. Not rage.
Worse.
Disappointment.
A silent verdict.

It just happens,
a full close-up,
like a slow zoom in a sad indie film.

And I evaporate on cue.
Right there.
I blink,
to will away the tears.
He blinks,
a single expression
that says:
"Seriously?"
The eye-narrow of *"Really?"*

He is younger.
Technically.
But somehow manages to carry

the weight of my bad decisions
like he is the older one
who has to explain me
to our parents
to society
to himself
in therapy, probably.

And I..
I am the older one.
Chronologically.
Which implies I should know better,
But also means I know exactly
how much his face twists
when I mess up.
Which is... often.

And so I cry.
Not because he scolds me..
he would never.
But from love.
Because he is my anchor.
My "do you think I'm a failure?"
for his "no, but you are dramatic."

And when he looks at me..
that look,

I believe I have failed.
Because I have.
Repeatedly.

I do not hate him for it.
I hate that look.
But worse,
I hate deserving it.

16. Plan B

I did not "choose" this, you see.
It was not a choice.
It was the path of least resistance,
I followed whatever was
less uphill.

Engineering? Too math-y, too precise.
Medicine? Too long, too tedious.
Law? Too loud, too argumentative.

I majored in convenience.
Minored in running away.
I mastered the art of detours,
side quests,
strategic naps.

And people,
those endless inquisitive souls,
ask "So what's next?"
and I say,
"Surprise me."

But now,
the road ahead is pitch black

and I'm holding a flashlight
with no batteries,
no map,
no guiding star.
and a dying phone
clinging to 4% courage.

Plan B?
This *is* Plan B,
the only plan that ever truly existed.
Plan A? A myth,
a little story I told to convince the world
I was stable,
or at least something resembling it.

And somehow,
I'm still here.
Not thriving.
Not crashing.

Just...
drifting.
Like a paper boat in a puddle,
dodging cigarette butts
and pretending it's the sea.

17. Dear Diary, You Useless B*tch

"Writing is healing," they say.
But *where*, I ask,
where does it heal?

I have bled my ache into art,
my panic poured into prose,
my spirals transformed into haikus,
and yet, I felt like trash.

I devoured Bukowski,
Rumi, Rupi.
I whispered "healing" into blank pages
and all the while,
the pages I scribbled on
turned their faces away.

Once, I even wrote a suicide note.
But, oh, the delicate artist in me,
edited it,
for tone, for rhythm.
Accidentally made it rhyme.
And then, the great absurdity..
I got distracted,

and ended up writing a blog post instead.

Turns out,
naming the wound
does not make it heal.

It only gives you insomnia,
imposter syndrome,
and the fine art of saying,
"I am processing,"
instead of the honest truth:
"I am completely unwell."

Yet, I write.
Not because it saves me.
No, not at all.
But because it is the only thing
that sits beside me quietly,
and lets me be
a little tragic,
with just enough style
to fool the world,
and maybe,
fool *myself.*

18. Strategic Collapse

This morning,
I rose with resolve.
 "Today, I will try."

I made a list.
I brushed my hair.
I opened the window
to let hope in.

I replied to emails.
I watered a plant that might already be dead.
I smiled at my reflection
with all the conviction.

Today, I said,
will not be like the others.
But of course,
it was.

Because by noon
I had opened tabs,
"Best way to disappear legally."
"How to tell if your ambition is dying or just tired."

By afternoon,
I had complimented someone
I do not like,
and resented it.

By evening,
I had talked myself out of joy..
again.
I declined the invitation.
I deleted the pitch.
I postponed the dream
out of sheer fear.

I did not mean to fail today.
I swear it.
I wore deodorant.
I meditated.
I tried that breathing thing.

I tried to win.
I really did.
But every time I got close
to becoming someone,
some strange part of me,
still clung to old grief.

And I believed her.

Because self-sabotage
wears the voice
of someone who sounds like
they're protecting you.

So here I am.
On the brink
of becoming,
but too familiar with the fall
to risk the flight.

Maybe tomorrow
I will try again.
Or maybe not.

19. Wrong Bus, Right Story

I boarded the wrong bus.
An actual, diesel-fueled
betrayal of Maps
and my own sense of direction,
which has been shaky
since birth.

Ten minutes in,
the scenery grew unfamiliar,
too green, too quiet.

I panicked,
of course.
Mildly.

The bus driver glanced at me
with the practiced apathy
of someone who's seen worse.

And then..
I stayed.

I thought,
why not?

What's one more wrong turn
in a life already mapped by detours?

So I rode.
To nowhere in particular.

An old man with a paper bag of oranges
told me about his dead cat
and, world politics.
A child handed me a melted candy
with the grace of a god.
A woman wept quietly in the shadows.
I did not ask,
but I understood.

The sun slanted across the window.
And for once,
I was not rushing to be
anywhere else.

The wrong bus
did not take me
to a revelation.
Only to a softer version
of being lost.
And perhaps,
that is all

I have ever needed.

I got off hours later.
Unchanged.

Still lost.
Still me.
But maybe now
with a story
no one asked for
and a kind of peace
that only comes
from having nothing
go *right*.

20. Oops. That Worked.

I barely managed to save the file.
The project. The deadline.
Myself.

I had but one task.
Missed the mark entirely.
And they say,
"Wow. That was bold."
Bold? No.
It was a mistake.

I called in sick to a meeting.
Someone else took my place.
They spoke.
They soared.
They now thrive.
You are welcome.

I ghosted a group project.
They won an award.
I did not attend the ceremony.
I did, however, read the article,
my name absent,
as it ought to be.

I dropped out of something
right when someone else stepped in
and called it destiny.
I love that for them.
I do.

My breakdown becomes
their breakthrough.
My offhand apology
the closure they needed
to forgive a father I have never met.

How thoroughly absurd,
that I fail with such
poetic accuracy,
that life rearranges itself
for others to rise?

No cape.
No cause.
Just me,
in yesterday's socks,
stumbling through life
with such disappointing grace
that the world rearranges itself
to accommodate the void I leave behind.

I have never won a thing.
But once,
in a moment too quiet to be dramatic,
someone said,
"Your quitting made me stay."
And I held that sentence
like a relic.

And perhaps
for people like myself,
this is what salvation looks like:

Accidental.
Invisible.
Undefinable.
And God help me
real.

21. Unwritten Ending

...

The emptiness becomes the poem.

Absence becomes presence.

The failure is the silence.

The world continues, grows, blooms, all around the void.

www.ingramcontent.com/pod-product-compliance
Lightning Source LLC
Chambersburg PA
CBHW070556160726
48003CB00005B/2073